PERSPECTIVES ON DIALOGUE

MAKING TALK DEVELOPMENTAL FOR INDIVIDUALS AND ORGANIZATIONS

PERSPECTIVES ON DIALOGUE

MAKING TALK DEVELOPMENTAL FOR INDIVIDUALS AND ORGANIZATIONS

Nancy M. Dixon

Center for Creative Leadership
Greensboro, North Carolina

The Center for Creative Leadership is an international, nonprofit educational institution founded in 1970 to foster leadership and effective management for the good of society overall. As a part of this mission, it publishes books and reports that aim to contribute to a general process of inquiry and understanding in which ideas related to leadership are raised, exchanged, and evaluated. The ideas presented in its publications are those of the author or authors.

The Center thanks you for supporting its work through the purchase of this volume. If you have comments, suggestions, or questions about any Center publication, please contact Walter W. Tornow, Vice President, Research and Publication, at the address given below.

Center for Creative Leadership
Post Office Box 26300
Greensboro, North Carolina 27438-6300

CENTER FOR CREATIVE LEADERSHIP°

©1996 Center for Creative Leadership

CCL No. 168

Library of Congress Cataloging-in-Publication Data

Dixon, Nancy M., 1937–
    Perspectives on dialogue : making talk developmental for individuals and organizations / Nancy M. Dixon.
        p. cm.
    Includes bibliographical references.
    ISBN 1-882197-16-X
    1. Communication in organizations. 2. Interpersonal communication. 3. Dialogue. 4. Critical thinking. 5. Communicative competence. I. Title.
HD30.3.D583 1996
302.3'5—dc20   95-50957
                                               CIP

Table of Contents

Preface vii

Acknowledgments ix

Introduction 1

Talk and Development 1

    Individual Development 2

    Organizational Development 3

    Development as a Necessary Response to Complexity 3

    Dialogue: Developmental Talk 5

Five Perspectives on Dialogue for Development 7

    Argyris: Organizational Learning 7

    Bohm: Developing Shared Meaning 10

    Mezirow: The Conditions for Rational Discourse 13

    Johnson and Johnson: Cooperation and Productivity 15

    Freire: Transformation 21

Practical Observations on Dialogue 24

    A Definition 24

    The Purpose of Dialogue 25

    The Role of Others in Learning 25

    People Already Know How to Have a Dialogue 28

    Dialogue Is a Relationship 28

    Dialogue Can Offset the Instrumental Nature of Work Relationships 29

    Dialogue Affirms the Intellectual Capability of Ordinary Human Beings 30

    The Outcome of Dialogue Is Unpredictable 31

    Dialogue Is Paradoxical 31

Examples of How Dialogue can be Incorporated into Work Processes 32

Conclusion 37

Appendix A 39

    Future Search Conferences 39

    Open Space Technology 39

    Action-learning 40

    Real-time Strategic Change 42

Appendix B: The Conditions of Dialogue 43

    Speech Acts 43

    Situation Variables 44

Bibliography 45

Preface

Perhaps like many authors, I have written this as much for myself as I have to communicate my ideas to others. For me writing has often been a way to clarify my own thinking or to make sense of a difficult issue with which I am wrestling. Dialogue fits well into my category of difficult issues.

I have been struck by the enthusiasm people express for dialogue. Over the last few years dialogue groups have formed around the country and dialogue seminars have sprung up. The term "dialogue" is now frequently heard when the speaker wants to convey that the discussion will be in greater depth or will be more real than usual. Yet, as I listen to conversations between organizational members or sit in meetings in organizations, I hear very little that I would call dialogue going on. It is the near absence of something we seem to find so appealing that perplexes me. Is it that we lack the skills to have a dialogue? Do we need more training courses in listening or communication? Or do we already know how to dialogue but are constrained by the organizations in which we function so that we are unable to do what we know how to do? I have resided on both sides of that quandary.

On the "we lack the necessary skills" side, I have given courses that teach Argyris' Model II skills for many years at the university. Although the skills are difficult to learn and can, at times, be very frustrating, these courses are, without doubt, the ones my students say they find most valuable. They learn a set of skills that they say impact not only their work life, but their personal life as well. I have been intrigued by the way change happens in those learners. They make a significant change not when they have mastered the technique, which can take up to a year, but when they have internalized the values represented in the technique. The skills themselves are like a door that allows them to reach the values.

On the side of "it's the situation that constrains us," for many years I led Great Books discussion groups. We didn't teach skills in how to dialogue in Great Books, but there were some strict rules we followed in those discussions such as: no one could talk unless he or she had read the book we were discussing; no one could reference an outside authority, we all spoke only from our own understanding of what we had read; the leader, who framed the questions under discussion, was limited to asking questions for which she truly had no answer herself. Those rules, and others, created the conditions which allowed a rich and meaningful dialogue to take place.

Having experienced both sides of the conundrum without finding a satisfying resolution, I have returned to many of the theorists who have influenced my thinking about dialogue to look for answers. As you will read, what I have come away with is a reframing of the issue that is based more in the way we relate to each other than with either our skill level or the conditions under which we employ them.

Acknowledgments

This paper has benefitted from the helpful review of many people. I would like to especially thank the following: Robert Burnside, Bill Drath, Cynthia Graham, Jack Mezirow, Charles Palus, James Rush, and Ellen Van Velsor.

Introduction

There is a growing sense today that organizations and the people that make them up are, to repeat a figure of speech recently used by Robert Kegan (1994), in over their heads. As diversity becomes the rule and change the sole constant, complexity is increasing. The only effective response to this complexity is development: both at the individual level and at the organizational level.

Consequently, a great deal of effort is now being devoted to individual and organizational development. One developmental activity, which is much practiced but imperfectly understood, takes place at the intersection between these levels: talk.

Not all talk is developmental, of course. In this paper I will first discuss the relationship between talk and development in organizations, looking at the basic ways that developmental talk—or, as it is often referred to, dialogue—differs from the skilled talk that goes on all the time. I will next summarize five perspectives on dialogue as offered by leading theorists, and then make a series of practical observations based on these views. Finally, I will review some examples of how dialogue has been incorporated into the work processes of organizations.

This paper is meant primarily for human resources professionals and practicing managers who are responsible for individual and organizational development, but it should also be of interest to anyone who is concerned with development.

Talk and Development

As a number of studies have documented (Kotter, 1990; Mintzberg, 1973; Stewart, 1985), talk is the most frequent activity of managers. Some say that as much as 75 percent of a manager's day is spent in conversation (for instance, Gronn, 1983).

Yet, for all this, there is a sense that something is wrong with the way people talk to each other at work—something is artificial, false, or at least unsatisfying much of the time. They often think to themselves that they have to be careful about what they say and to whom they say it. There are things that might be said privately, to a trusted colleague, that cannot be said publicly. On the other hand, people sometimes say something publicly that they realize they do not really believe; it is said "just for show." Organizational talk often has a game-like quality that makes it seem unreal.

I believe that people long for a more authentic kind of interaction with their co-workers but that they are not sure that it is possible, or even if their longing is legitimate. Work is not generally thought of as a place where you are supposed to get your own needs met. Thus, people come to accept what they believe to be inevitable, that they must leave a part of themselves at home when they come to work.

What is lost, when talk is limited in these ways, are two kinds of development: Individuals lose the opportunity to learn in ways that could foster their growth—if they cannot *be* themselves at work, they cannot *develop* themselves at work—and the organization, the system as a whole, loses the opportunity to learn those things about itself and about its interaction with its environment that could lead to its development.

Individual Development

There is substantial agreement among development theorists that individual development is, potentially, lifelong rather than ending with adulthood. Although these theorists differ greatly about what comprises various stages, or even if stages are an appropriate frame, they generally agree about the direction that adult development takes (Commons, Richards, & Armon, 1984; Kegan, 1994; Labouvie-Vief, 1984; Perry, 1970): Given both challenge and support, individual adults take on an increasingly more open, differentiated, and integrated perspective. *Open,* in this context, means a willingness to entertain alternative perspectives; *differentiated* means the individual is able to draw finer distinctions between concepts (for example, the concept of "team" can be differentiated into self-directed and manager-led or, alternatively, into task teams, performing teams, production teams, and so on, each having distinguishing characteristics that result in different issues); and *integrated* means that the individual is able to weave these differences into an increasingly complex whole, a system view rather than an ethnocentric or fragmented view. As an individual becomes more developed he or she is able to deal with increasing complexity—or, perhaps more accurately, is able to construct increasingly more complex perspectives on the world. The opposite of continued adult development is rigid and highly defended thought patterns—patterns that leave a person less able to adapt to changing conditions and less able to change.

Adult development is, however, only a potential; it is not a certainty. For development to occur an individual must continue to face new issues or problems for which current responses are inadequate. In order to deal with new challenges the person must reframe his or her understanding of "self in the world" or "self in relation to the system" of which the individual is a part.

It is, of course, quite distressing to find that one's current understanding of "self in the world" is inadequate, that one doesn't yet "have it figured out." So an individual in the midst of development must have the support of others, both to sustain the effort and to offer alternative frames.

Organizations, however, are in general poor places to develop. People can develop specialization in them: There are adequate challenges and support for reframing within an area of technical skill or abstract concepts. But when it comes to developing themselves more broadly, the way people talk to each other (avoiding open exchange, trying to win at all costs, and other tendencies described below) can prevent them from receiving the information and support that is necessary for reframing.

Organizational Development

Organizations also acquire patterns of interaction that can make it difficult for the system as a whole to find out about itself and thus to develop. Chris Argyris (1990) has referred to these patterns as "defensive routines": customary ways of acting that the organization evolves to avoid embarrassment or conflict. For example, people frequently modify information that is sent upward through the organization so that it appears more favorable, and subordinates often agree to do a task or carry out a process that they believe will not work. Defensive routines work in the sense that they *do* prevent embarrassment and conflict, but in so doing they also prevent the organization from learning about challenges which, if faced directly, could lead to new ways of thinking—that is, could lead to development.

I believe that both individual and organizational development are dependent upon learning and that learning is dependent upon talk; thus, talk leads to learning, which leads to development. Obviously, though, not all talk leads to learning. As I have just pointed out, some talk may indeed work against it. (It is also important to note that learning can and does occur without talk—for example, learning calculus from a computer program, learning history from a text. However, the learning I am interested in in this paper is the kind I referenced above: learning that results in an individual or system reframing self in relation to the world.)

Development as a Necessary Response to Complexity

Kegan (1994) has defined development as the "active process of increasingly organizing the relationship of the self to the environment. The relationship gets better organized by increasing differentiations of the self from the environment and thus by increasing integrations of the environment"

(p. 114). At a systems level, Ashby's (1957, 1960) law of requisite variety, which states that the internal regulatory mechanisms of a system must be as diverse as the environment with which it is trying to deal, is again an argument for differentiation and integration—or the development of the organization as an ever-more-complex system.

To live in a world that is culturally diverse requires individuals to be more complex than to live in a homogeneous world. People face diversity every day as organizations become more heterogeneous and struggle with ensuing issues of equity and fairness. The women and people of color who are exiting corporations in increasing numbers speak to the current ineptitude in addressing the complexity that cultural diversity brings with it (Barrentine, 1993). As organizations become more global, people must deal with yet wider issues of cultural diversity: fairness in wages and benefits within poorer countries, disruption of family patterns in traditional countries, and economic exploitation juxtaposed against national loyalty, to name only a few.

To live in a fast-changing environment requires greater complexity than to live in a more stable world. The speed with which product decisions must be made often prevents considered thought of their consequences. The technological advances that make possessions quickly obsolete create environmental problems and issues of equity about the use of the planet's scarce resources. The organizational changes that force people to frequently change tasks, colleagues, and location leave them bereft of community and support. Einstein's insight that the world that people have made as a result of the level of thinking they have done thus far creates problems that cannot be solved at the same level as they were created makes the case for development.

This is an age in which people are aware that their truths are embedded within a paradigm that, over time, will surely be transcended. This consciousness requires more complexity than living in a world in which truth is sure and steadfast. Some have said that this may be the first generation that is fully aware that it functions within a paradigm—that knowledge is ephemeral and conditional. Theorists such as Thomas Kuhn (1962) and Peter Berger (1966) have carefully illustrated how people construct their own reality. That is a difficult fate—to not have truth—to labor in the great vineyard of constructed reality. It requires much greater complexity than many have been able to develop. Robert Kegan (1994) was right: People find themselves in over their heads much of the time.

The organizations in which people work are also in over their heads. They are actively searching for new ways of acting and interacting. There is a growing acknowledgment that organizations cannot face this increased level of complexity armed with the traditional tools of bureaucracy: control, consistency, and predictability (Block, 1993). Organizations are actively seeking new ways of interacting, such as empowerment, self-directed teams, and organizational learning. They are, as well, seeking new forms of structure—for instance, Handy's (1989) shamrock organization and Ackoff's (1994) democratic corporation.

Individual and organizational development is a long-term answer to dealing with increased complexity, not a quick fix. Development moves at its own pace. It can be stifled, as it regularly is in current organizations, but it is difficult to hurry. The best that can be done is to make organizations places where individuals can know themselves and speak their truth.

Dialogue: Developmental Talk

I suggested above that if people cannot *be* themselves at work, they cannot *develop* themselves at work. They may fail to be themselves by (1) misleading others in what they say, (2) saying more than they know, or (3) saying nothing. Being oneself at work means that the person speaks authentically, agreeing and disagreeing, voicing one's hopes and distresses. Individual development is about taking on an increasingly open, differentiated, and integrated perspective. To do that the person must give voice to his or her current perspective so that others can respond to it. Then in talking with others, reflecting an authentic self, the person learns from others about his or her tacit assumptions and, if those assumptions prove to be no longer viable, may choose to change them—to develop. Thus, speaking out of one's own experience, he or she may hear that experience affirmed by others, perhaps in more eloquent words, and come to understand it more fully—to develop. Similarly, the person can internalize the perspectives of others, and integrate their ideas with his or her own—develop. Carl Jung (1963, p. 3) said, "I can only make direct statements, only 'tell stories.' Whether or not the stories are 'true' is not the problem. The only question is whether what I tell is *my* fable, *my* truth." Developmental talk requires each person to say one's own truth—not *the* truth but one's own truth. And in giving voice to that truth, each person opens the door to his or her development.

I do not want to be misunderstood as advocating that people should say everything that comes into their heads, that they should be "brutally honest." I am not suggesting that it is necessary to give voice to every thought in order to be authentic or to develop. It is, however, necessary to speak authentically and fully about all which bears upon the subject of the dialogue. To do less is to mislead others who are trying to learn, and to prevent oneself from learning as well.

Another way people can limit their development is by saying more than they know. It is difficult to avoid this, particularly when a person is placed in an authority role by virtue of position or expertise. Morris Cohen, in speaking facetiously about professors, once said, "No man, however conservative, can stand before a class day after day and refrain from saying more than he knows." I could paraphrase that to say, "No manager, however conservative, can talk with subordinates day after day and refrain from saying more than he or she knows." When individuals say more than they know they lose the ability to hear the perspectives of others, and others, hearing that person's certainty, refrain from offering their conflicting thoughts, which might widen and enrich his or her perspective. Freire reminded us of the need for humility in talking with each other when he said, "The encounter of men addressed to the common task of learning and acting . . . is broken if the parties (or one of them) lack humility. How can I [talk developmentally with others] if I always project ignorance onto others and never perceive my own?" In developmental talk one is not obliged to say more than he or she knows; the task is not to convince, sell, or get "buy in." A person can, even as a manager or expert, speak his or her own truth, without claiming it as *the* truth.

Silence, which in practical terms is the opposite of saying more than one knows, is equally dehabilitating to development. Audre Lorde (1984), the black feminist poet, has written eloquently about silence: "I have come to believe over and over again that what is most important to me must be spoken, made verbal and shared, even at the risk of having it bruised or misunderstood. That the speaking profits me, beyond any other effect" (p. 40). People break their silence because it profits them, in their own growth and development and in the development of others.

People become what they act out, conditioning themselves by their play acting. If, day by day, they act indifferent when they really hurt for others, disinterested when they are truly ashamed, stoical when inside they are joyous, then, over time, they will become indifferent, disinterested, and stoical. If, on the other hand, the situation is such that they can act authentically, openly, and in relationship with others, then they have the opportunity to develop into authentic, open people who deal with others in relationship and not as objects.

The kind of talk that I have just described has been called *dialogue*. There are a number of theorists who have thought very carefully about the nature of dialogue. Let's review their ideas and see what can be learned from them about how people might talk in more meaningful ways at work.

Five Perspectives on Dialogue for Development

The five frameworks for dialogue reviewed here are based on the work of Chris Argyris, David Bohm, David Johnson and Roger Johnson, Jack Mezirow, and Paulo Freire. Each approaches dialogue from a different discipline; thus collectively, they afford the possibility of a richer and more complex understanding of a way to talk with each other than might be gained from only one perspective. You will certainly note differences among the five, as well as underlying commonalities. I invite you in reading through these to stay open to differing perspectives, to differentiate the concepts, and, at the end, to attempt with me to integrate the ideas into a meaningful whole.

Argyris: Organizational Learning

Chris Argyris has for twenty years been steadfast in his conviction that organizational members can learn to interact in ways that improve their own and their organization's learning. Through extensive data collection of some 6,000 cases, Argyris has found that organizational members consistently interact in ways that limit rather than facilitate their own learning. This "normal" way of interacting, which he has referred to as Model I, is characterized by such strategies as: (1) asking questions in such a way as to get the other person to agree with one's own view, (2) advocating one's own view in a manner that limits others' questioning of it, and (3) privately evaluating the other person's view and attributing causes to it.

These and similar strategies are intended to persuade others to one's point of view, to minimize any negative feelings that may arise, and to appear rational and reasonable. Such goals do not seem inappropriate; it is, however, apparent how such strategies can limit learning. For example, if the questions I ask are designed to get the other person to agree with my own view, they will do little to elicit the other person's view. Thus, I will not learn how the other person reasons about the situation nor how the other's view may differ from my own. When I advocate my own view in a way that discourages others' questioning it, if my view is wrong, I will not be able to discover that. Likewise, when I privately evaluate the other's view and privately attribute cause to it, I cannot determine if my evaluation is accurate or if the attributions I make are correct. In other words, although each of these strategies may be effective in my "winning," they severely limit my learning.

Argyris has pointed out that people have a tendency to draw inferences very quickly from what they see and hear. This is done with such speed that they are often not aware that the conclusions they have reached are inferences, and moreover they quickly lose track of the data (what was said or done) that caused them to draw the inference. The ability to quickly draw inferences serves people well; it is a critical part of intelligence and effectiveness in functioning in a fast-paced world. But it also gets them into trouble. Because people tend to see their conclusions as "truth" or accurate, no effort is made to check them out—people make an hypothesis, sometimes on the basis of quite scanty data, and proceed to function on it as though it were true. For example, someone may infer that a frown means that the boss does not want to hear a different perspective, or that Fred's being late so many times means he is not very interested in the job, or that the group expects new members to just listen and not contribute.

The set of interaction practices (Model II skills) that Argyris suggested are a way to overcome the negative consequences of the tendency to quickly draw inferences from scanty data include: (1) actively inquiring into the other's views and the reasoning that supports them; (2) advocating one's own view and reasoning in a way that encourages others to confront it and to help the speaker discover where the view may be mistaken; and (3) publicly stating the inferences that one makes about others and the data that leads to those inferences, and inviting others to correct the inferences if they are inaccurate.

Using such strategies, people may discover more adequate views than those they began with. With the help of others, individuals may also uncover assumptions that they were unaware of and which will afford them the opportunity to test whether those assumptions are valid. As Argyris has pointed out many times, people require others to help them discover, invent, and especially produce new actions.

However, people will have to give up some of their goals in order to interact using Model II strategies. For example, a person will "win" using Model II strategies only if his or her reasoning and conclusions are in fact not fallacious. There is the risk of losing. There is the risk of being embarrassed if one's view is inaccurate, and the risk of embarrassing others if their views are not supported by their reasoning. When a person gives up the strategies that prevent others from expressing negative feelings, he or she risks having to experience those feelings.

Although Model II strategies are easily stated, they are very difficult to implement; they engage ingrained patterns for protecting oneself from embarrassment and threat. Those ingrained patterns automatically produce certain behaviors. For example, a person can ask "leading" questions and make inferences about other people without even realizing it; people may unwittingly design ways to state their views so that they are untestable, to prevent the embarrassment of discovering they are wrong.

To become skilled at interacting using Model II strategies individuals must: (1) identify the learning-limiting behaviors that they currently use, (2) uncover the tacit assumptions that mediate those behaviors, (3) alter those assumptions and design appropriate new behaviors, and (4) practice those new behaviors until they become automatic.

The first and second steps are greatly facilitated by others. Because meaning structures often may be tacit and related behavior automatic, they are difficult, if not impossible, to recognize in oneself. They are often, however, readily apparent to others.

For Model II skills to be developed, these steps must be engaged in repeatedly, as subsequent learning-limiting behaviors and tacit meaning structures are uncovered. To become skillful enough to use Model II skills in situations of even mild threat takes considerable time: Argyris has said up to a year before behavior becomes automatic enough to use in situations of mild threat.

One way to facilitate the process of learning Model II skills is to ask a person to write about a difficult situation that he or she would have preferred to have handled better. The page is divided horizontally into two columns. In the right-hand column, the person records, as accurately as possible, the conversation that occurred in the course of the situation. In the left-hand column, the person records the thoughts and feelings that he or she had but did not express during the conversation. The case is then analyzed by a group of colleagues who are also attempting to learn the Model II skill set. The case analysis is both an opportunity for the group to practice the Model II skills themselves and an opportunity to assist the case writer in identifying the ways that the person may have limited his or her own learning.

In the aggregate the cases can provide useful insight into the defensive routines that limit the learning of the organization. Argyris (1993) has also developed a corresponding interview process that is useful in collecting data related to defensive routines. The defensive routines are displayed in causal maps that can be confirmed or disconfirmed by organizational stakeholders.

Argyris has acknowledged that Model II interaction is normative, not value-free; it is not a set of interaction skills that one could use as the means to achieve any given end. The normative end is, in fact, learning. The claim Argyris made for Model II skills is that the use of the skill set increases the amount of learning that results from the interaction. Learning, then, is the goal of Model II and its highest value.

There are values embedded within the three governing variables that Argyris articulates for Model II: valid information, free and informed choice, and internal commitment to the choice.

When in conversation with others, people typically state their conclusions but less frequently offer the original data that led to those conclusions. In using the term *valid information,* Argyris implied that people need to offer others both their conclusions and the original data that led them to those conclusions. Valid information gives others the opportunity to determine for themselves whether the data warrant the conclusion.

Valid information further requires that people make a concerted effort to gain directly observable data and reasoning from others. Then both parties have valid information. Finally, *complete* data must be offered, as opposed to withholding certain elements that might influence the other in ways the speaker would not prefer. Valid information requires that people make available to others *all* of the relevant data and that they report the data as accurately as they can. Underlying the idea of valid information is the scientific concept of a "community of inquiry guided by such norms as intersubjectively verifiable data, explicit inferences, and public falsifiability" (Argyris, Putnam, & Smith, 1985).

The second and third governing variables, free and informed choice and internal commitment to that choice, are both based upon the first. For a choice to be informed, the individual must have all of the relevant information; for it to be free, the individual must not be coerced or make the choice out of fear or even because of the anticipation of extrinsic rewards. If someone agrees with another's opinion because he or she anticipates that the agreement will gain favor with that person, a free choice has not been made. A person makes a free and informed choice when the data support the choice, the logic is reasonable to him or her, and the choice is in concert with his or her own objectives and values. Internal commitment is a natural outgrowth of free and informed choice. People are most likely to be committed to those choices they make freely.

Bohm: Developing Shared Meaning

In contrast to Argyris' Model II idea, David Bohm's concept of dialogue is relatively technique-free. Despite this, the two ideas are surprisingly similar in terms of the goal toward which they strive: to uncover and examine the tacit theories-in-use (which Bohm referred to as "programs") that mediate actions.

Bohm (1985) was a theoretical physicist, professor at the University of London, and a fellow of the Royal Society. His ideas of dialogue grew out of his experience and knowledge of physics; he described the world as an "unbroken flowing whole." He provided compelling evidence from quantum physics for this view, contrasting it with the more mechanistic view of

Newtonian physics and with the earlier Aristotelian view of the world as an integral organism. Yet Bohm acknowledged that quantum physics is also a "view" and, as with previous views, is ultimately based on a leap of faith. The starting point of any view is metaphysical, and only beyond that initial leap of faith is it based in logic or science. Thus he held his own view as a "program" to be continually examined and questioned. He said, "We have to have enough faith in our world-view to work from it, but not that much faith that we think it's the final answer" (Bohm, 1985, p. 4).

According to Bohm, people typically deal with the world not as a whole but as though it were multiple fragments, one fragment being unrelated to others. His objection to a fragmentary view of the world was that it disposes people to think of the divisions between things as absolute and final rather than as having a limited utility and validity. Holding a fragmentary view, the person begins to act on the world as though it were indeed fragmented and in so doing creates a fragmented world that seems to exist independent of his or her actions. To use Argyris' term, people create a situation that is "self-sealing." A fragmentary view of the world is exemplified, for example, in viewing the boundaries of countries as authentic or manifest. Such a view makes it possible to see the people of France and Germany as two entities rather than people divided by an arbitrarily drawn line, a line that, given different conditions, might be placed very differently. When the mechanistic explanation of reality is taken to its ultimate implication, people are left with a universe which is basically indifferent to humankind and in which there is meaning only to the extent that individuals can construct meaning in their own eyes. It is this fragmentary view of the world that Bohm hoped to overcome through dialogue.

Society, to work, must be based on shared meaning, which Bohm likened to the cement that holds society together. At present, society has an incoherent set of meanings, a poor quality cement, so it is falling apart. His goal, then, was to develop not higher individual intelligence but higher social intelligence. The first task in creating such shared meanings is simply to apprehend the meanings of others. That, in and of itself, will bring a certain order. Bohm said that dialogue is a way to apprehend the meaning of others and to thereby experience the wholeness of the world rather than the fragments into which understanding is broken.

Bohm (1990) contrasted dialogue with discussion. *Dialogue* comes from the Greek word *dialogos,* meaning "through"; dialogue is like a stream running between two banks. He noted that it is the stream that counts; the banks merely give form to the stream. The stream is analogous to the free flow of meaning between people. *Discussion,* on the other hand, has the same root word as *percussion* or *concussion,* meaning "to break things apart or to analyze." Discussion leads to separate points of view; dialogue leads to shared meaning.

Bohm referred to the products of thinking as "programs." People are unaware of these programs, not of their content but of their nature. The programs people construct appear to them to be in some sense reality or truth. Bohm pointed out that thinking (the production of programs) is a slow process whereas the recall and use of programs is swift. Thinking cannot keep up with thought (programs). Thus the programs that people have constructed cannot be changed through thinking alone.

Bohm compared these programs to the bright lights of Las Vegas. The lights, in their nearness, prevent people from knowing or seeing the stars beyond the lights. The lights constitute reality, blotting out the larger universe. If the lights are "dissolved," then the stars appear and that new reality is apparent. Bohm suggested that dialogue is a way to uncover and "dissolve" programs.

Bohm's concerns about the pervasiveness of programs made him unwilling even to specify the conditions of productive dialogue, seeing such conditions themselves as "programs" that have to be examined. According to him, "One of the difficulties is that the thoughts contain all sorts of presuppositions which limit us and hold us in rigid grooves. What we have to do is discover these presuppositions and get rid of them—get free of them. I don't think that we can establish conditions for a dialogue, except to say that we both want to make a dialogue" (1985, p. 37).

His guidance for dialogue, then, is minimal. To create a dialogue requires a group that will meet without purpose or a specified goal so that its members can talk freely. The group needs to be large enough that subcultures can develop within it. In a small group, Bohm said, people can hide their deeper ideas through politeness and avoidance; in a large group, of twenty or thirty people, subgroups will form and raise the deeper issues. But he noted that, as soon as people try to talk about things that are of such importance, they get excited and quit hearing each other.

Bohm suggested that participants in dialogue suspend their assumptions —that is, that they consider what both their and others' assumptions mean without judging or attempting to come to any compromise. When all the participants in a group agree to suspend their assumptions and attempt to apprehend the meanings of others, they are already in the act of sharing meaning. Bohm said it is not necessary that everyone hold the same opinions for shared meaning to emerge, that the joint agreement to apprehend the meaning of others is more important than the content of the opinions and assumptions themselves. "When you listen to somebody else, whether you like it or not, what they say becomes part of you" (Bohm, 1992, p. 119). So in a dialogue everybody's ideas are held by all. There is a common pool of information. Out of this social intelligence comes something new.

It is holding on to assumptions and defending them that get in the way of dialogue. He eschewed persuasion and attempts to convince others, maintaining that if something is right there is no need for persuasion. "Truth," said Bohm (1990, p. 22), "does not emerge from opinions; it must emerge from something else—perhaps from a more free movement of this tacit mind."

Bohm suggested that dialogue be an exchange that is conducted without an agenda and without a leader. He used the analogy of an empty space in which anything may come in. In describing dialogue, Bohm related a story about a North American Indian tribe of hunter-gatherers. From time to time the whole tribe would come together in a circle and talk. No one appeared to have called the meeting or to have led it; the group made no decisions and seemingly had no agenda. Yet when the meeting ended people knew what to do because they now understood each other. They might then get together in small groups and make plans or decide to do something.

Bohm realized that dialogue is not easy. It is difficult to hear an assumption that contradicts one's own; it is difficult to see some people dominating the dialogue while others say nothing. As with Argyris' Model II skills, a certain vulnerability is demanded. "An idea must be vulnerable—you have to be ready to drop it, just as the person who holds the idea must be vulnerable, I think. He should not identify with it" (Bohm, 1985, p. 40).

Mezirow: The Conditions for Rational Discourse

Jack Mezirow (1991) has described himself as an adult educator, coming out of the emancipatory tradition of Paulo Freire and Saul Alinsky. His hope is that, through learning and reflection, adults can free themselves of what William Blake in his poem "London" called "mind-forg'd manacles." As did Argyris and Bohm, Mezirow has pointed out the need for adults to help each other uncover their tacit assumptions. Mezirow's focus has been more individual than the other theorists. I include his concepts here because he has provided clear guidance about the conditions under which dialogue can occur and because he has differentiated that which can be validated through proof from that which must rely on dialogue for validation.

Drawing heavily on the work of Jurgen Habermas, Mezirow (1991) framed three kinds of learning, one of which, "communicative" learning, requires interaction with others of the type discussed above. It will be helpful first to differentiate the three types and then to explain why communicative learning requires dialogue.

The most familiar type of learning described by Mezirow is "instrumental"—that is, learning that leads to the control and manipulation of the environment, which in this definition includes other people. Instrumental learning is based in empirical knowledge and involves predictions about observable events. It involves cause-and-effect relationships that can be proven or disproved. Knowledge is produced by testing hypotheses that lead to greater control over situations. Quality control is an application of instrumental learning.

Communicative learning is associated with the practical rather than the empirical. It is learning to understand what others mean and to make oneself understood. The goal of communicative learning is to gain insight and to reach common understanding rather than to control. Most of the problems and issues people deal with in organizations fall into this category, including intentions, social concepts, politics, reasons, feelings, and beliefs.

Using communicative learning, one cannot "prove" something with empirical evidence. It cannot, for example, be proven that Jones would be the best person to fill the vice-president slot or that a report has sufficient depth to satisfy a client's needs. According to Mezirow (1991, p. 76), "We are continually confronted with having to determine the validity of reports, predictions, explanations, arguments, and denials as well as the implicit claims of validity involved in justifying commands, requests, excuses, and recommendations."

With communicative learning, validity can be determined in one of two ways. The first is to rely on force, tradition, or authority, as in a religious dogma or the rights of kings. The second way is to rely on a broad consensus of those who are informed, rational, and objective. But even here the idea is not one of simply voting but rather an opinion that is reached through a deliberation in which each person has the opportunity to hear, influence, and challenge others. Consensual validation is based on the assumption that any unbiased group that had available to them the same information would arrive at a similar conclusion. It is the assumption at the heart of the Enlightenment: that the human mind is capable of using logic and reason to understand the world rather than having to rely on the interpretation of someone who claims authority through force, tradition, or divine right.

Consensual validation is recognizable as the process employed in a jury of peers. A group of objective individuals reviews the evidence and arguments and renders a decision, which, hopefully, is the same as another jury would render hearing the same evidence. Although less formalized in most situations, the same principles apply; people believe something is valid if, after examining the available data, a group of reasonable individuals comes to a consensus.

Because consensus may also be reached through coercion, it is necessary to construct standards related to objectivity. According to Mezirow (1991, pp. 77-78), those include: (1) Have accurate and complete information. (2) Be free from coercion and distorting self-deception. (3) Be able to weigh evidence and assess arguments objectively. (4) Be open to alternative perspectives. (5) Be able to become critically reflective upon presuppositions and their consequences. (6) Have equal opportunity to participate (including the chance to challenge, question, refute, and reflect and to hear others do the same). (7) Be able to accept an informed, objective, and rational consensus as a legitimate test of validity.

The third type of learning is "emancipatory." The goal of emancipatory learning is to identify and reflect on distorted meaning perspectives. Mezirow has pointed out, as did Bohm (in his view of programs), that individuals understand the world through a frame that they have constructed and that frame is often distorted by institutional, linguistic, and environmental forces that have been taken for granted by the individual. An example might be that women cannot succeed in upper management or that wealthy people should have greater protection under the law than the poor. Emancipatory learning is achieved through critical self-reflection but, as with Bohm's concept of dissolving programs, requires others to provide perspective.

It is Mezirow's (1991) concern that people have taken instrumental learning as the model for all learning and that they fail to understand that only instrumental learning can be validated through empirical means. For all other learning people must rely on each other and on establishing conditions that assist their ability to think together rationally.

Mezirow has focused on the individual and the ways institutions—including government, corporations, and educational organizations—impart distorting assumptions to the individual. His goal has been to free the individual of such assumptions through critical reflection; to do that he or she must also make institutions aware of their tacit assumptions.

Johnson and Johnson: Cooperation and Productivity

David Johnson and Roger Johnson (1989) are the foremost researchers on the relationship among learning, cooperation, and productivity. They have based their work on Morton Deutsch's (1949) theory of social inter-dependence. Over the last twenty years they have conducted more than forty studies to understand the conditions for and the outcomes of cooperation, particularly as it relates to learning. In addition they have conducted a meta-analysis of a hundred years of research with over five hundred studies related to this topic. Much of Johnson and Johnson's own work has been conducted in educational settings, although confirmation of their findings has involved all sectors. The conclusions presented here are primarily drawn from their meta-analysis.

There are three ways individuals can take action: cooperatively, competitively, and independently. Through cooperative action, individuals promote the success of others; through competitive action, they obstruct the success of others; independent action has no affect on others' success. Each of these three types of action can be understood as forms of social interdependence.[†]

Although Johnson and Johnson have said much about all three conditions, I will limit my discussion to their findings on cooperation, because it is that situation in which dialogue is critical. Four benefits of cooperative action are supported in their meta-analysis: productivity, reasoning strategies, process gain, and transfer of learning.

Productivity. In the more than 185 studies that have compared the impact of cooperative and competitive situations on achievement, the evidence is overwhelming that greater productivity is attained through cooperation. When cooperative situations are contrasted with individualistic situations (226 studies), the results are similar. These findings hold for both individual achievement and a total group's achievement.

Reasoning strategies. A second benefit is the improved quality of reasoning strategies that individuals employ in a cooperative situation. Reasoning strategies include, for example, integrating new information with prior knowledge, identifying concepts underlying data, problem solving, and metaphoric reasoning. The use of such strategies is increased in cooperative situations as well as the quality of the strategies themselves. In addition, metacognition, or knowledge about one's thinking processes, is more frequently in evidence in cooperative situations than it is in competitive or independent situations. Metacognition is critical because it leads to the generalized improvement in learning capability.

[†] According to Johnson and Johnson (1989, p. 23), "Social interdependence exists when the outcomes of individuals are affected by each other's actions. There are two types of social interdependence (cooperative and competitive) and the absence of social interdependence (individualistic efforts)."

Process gain. A third benefit is process gain—that is, in cooperative situations, new ideas or solutions are generated which would not have occurred if individuals were working independently. Again, there is significantly more process gain through cooperative situations than either competitive or independent situations.

Transfer of learning. The final benefit noted in this meta-analysis is transfer of learning. By "transfer of learning," Johnson and Johnson meant what an individual learned in the group situation that he or she is able to use in another situation, one that no longer involves the original group. The transfer finding is most significant when the knowledge gained is at a higher rather than lower cognitive level. With low-level cognitive knowledge there is little difference in whether the learning took place independently, competitively, or cooperatively. However, with more complex understandings, cooperative situations produce greater transfer.

Conditions for Positive Outcomes from Cooperation. These four findings, drawn from hundreds of studies, provide strong evidence that cooperative situations produce greater learning and achievement than do competitive or independent situations. Not all cooperation is effective, however, as anyone who has participated in a group situation can attest. The benefits described above do not occur by simply putting organizational members in a group and instructing them to reach a given outcome. There are a number of ways in which such benefits may be derailed in a group situation—for example, some members may do less than their share of the work, a free-rider effect; members who are viewed as having greater expertise or authority may be deferred to; and groups may create dysfunctional divisions of labor and certain individuals may dominate the interaction. Thus, it is only under certain conditions that cooperative efforts achieve the beneficial outcomes: (1) positive interdependence, (2) social skills, and (3) promotive interaction. It is the third of these that requires dialogue. Before discussing promotive interaction, I must frame that critical factor in terms of the other two.

Positive interdependence. Positive interdependence implies that individuals are linked with others in a way that one cannot achieve without others achieving as well. Moreover, in order to achieve the outcome, each individual must coordinate his or her activities with others. Simply being a member of a group does not automatically lead to higher levels of achievement, nor does group discussion alone, nor does a mere exchange of information; there must also be positive interdependence. For positive interdependence to exist, all individuals must be oriented toward an outcome (outcome interdependence) and the means through which that outcome is reached—such as resources, roles, and tasks—must be interdependent (means interdependence) as well.

Social skills. Cooperation requires individuals who are skilled in interpersonal and small-group interaction. Such skills might include conflict resolution, communication, trust-building, and decision making, to name a few. The group must periodically reflect on how well it is interacting and on what it might do to improve the way the group is functioning. It is clear, however, that social skills in the absence of positive interdependence and promotive interaction do not increase productivity and achievement.

Promotive interaction. Johnson and Johnson (1989, p. 63) defined promotive interaction as "individuals encouraging and facilitating each other's efforts to achieve, complete tasks, and produce in order to reach the group's goals." The interaction is described as "face to face" and although electronic or other technologically mediated interaction may produce the same results, that has not been tested through these studies.

All three of the conditions of cooperation are necessary for increased productivity and achievement; however, of the three, promotive interaction is clearly the most critical. Johnson and Johnson (1989, p. 63) described nine elements of promotive interaction: (1) providing each other with efficient and effective help and assistance, (2) exchanging needed resources such as information and materials and processing information more efficiently and effectively, (3) providing each other with feedback in order to improve subsequent performance of assigned tasks and responsibilities, (4) challenging each other's conclusions and reasoning in order to promote higher-quality decision making and greater insight into the problems being considered, (5) advocating the exertion of effort to achieve mutual goals, (6) influencing each other's efforts to achieve the group's goals, (7) acting in trusting and trustworthy ways, (8) being motivated to strive for mutual benefit, and (9) having a moderate level of arousal characterized by low anxiety and stress.

Many of these elements are self-explanatory; however, it may be useful to expand on some of these.

Information exchange and cognitive processes. Individuals exchange their data, conclusions, reasoning, and questions with others in promotive interaction. Although the cognitive benefits to the receiver of such an exchange are apparent, there is evidence that it is the speaker who makes the greatest cognitive gains from the exchange. Recent studies have shown that the act of orally summarizing information works to strengthen the speaker's understanding of that information. Such a finding would seem to bear out the insight of the Roman philosopher who said "Qui docet descit" (Whoever teaches, learns twice). Individuals organize information differently if they are going to present it to others than if they are trying to understand it solely for their own use. It is in the act of speaking that people tend to cognitively organize what they know.

A second beneficial action to the speaker is perspective-taking—that is, the act of paraphrasing the ideas and arguments of others. Perspective-taking is more than just being able to play back others' argument in order to check with them for accuracy. It is the ability to comprehend and voice how the situation appears from another's standpoint. Perspective-taking is the opposite of egocentrism—in which the individual is locked into a single view of the situation and is unaware of the limitations of that view or that other viable views may exist.

When one voices the perspective of another, that action inclines the other to disclose information more fully than if the perspective were not voiced. The additional information and the fuller comprehension of another perspective both work to increase the development of new knowledge on a complex issue. It is necessary, however, to hold both one's own and others' perspectives in mind at the same time to create new knowledge. Simply listening to another's perspective is less facilitative of the creation of new knowledge than is the actual voicing of the other's perspective. People place such a high value on information that it is almost counterintuitive to realize that the amount of actual information within a group is less important in reaching a high-quality solution to a problem than is actually voicing others' perspectives.

Having placed the emphasis here on the speaker rather than on the receiver of information, I should at least acknowledge that the receiver also benefits cognitively. In particular, the receiver is able to incorporate the knowledge, skills, and reasoning of others into his or her own understanding.

Controversy. When promotive interaction occurs, an unavoidable outcome is controversy. When managed constructively, controversy promotes uncertainty about one's own views, which leads to an active search for information, resulting in the reorganization of one's understanding. The constructive, rather than a destructive, management of controversy depends upon the group's social skills.

Controversy, as the term is used here, "exists when one person's ideas, information, conclusions, theories, and opinions are incompatible with those of another, and the two seek to reach agreement" (Johnson & Johnson, 1989, p. 87). Embedded within this definition are positive outcome and means interdependence. The outcome interdependence is the hoped for agreement and the means interdependence is different information.

Controversy leads to increased productivity through the following process (adapted from Johnson & Johnson, 1989, pp. 91-92):

(1) When individuals are presented with a problem or decision, they hold an initial conclusion based on categorizing and organizing incomplete information, their limited experiences, and their specific perspectives.

(2) As each individual presents his or her conclusion and its rationale to others, the person engages in cognitive rehearsal, deepening the understanding of his or her position, and discovers higher-level reasoning strategies.

(3) When the person is confronted by other people with different conclusions based on their information, experiences, and perspectives, he or she becomes uncertain as to the correctness of his or her views. A state of conceptual conflict or disequilibrium is created.

(4) Uncertainty, conceptual conflict, and disequilibrium motivate an active search for more information, new experiences, and a more adequate cognitive perspective and reasoning process in hopes of resolving the uncertainty.

(5) As the person adapts his or her cognitive perspectives and reasoning through understanding and accommodating the perspectives and reasoning of others, a new, reconceptualized, and reorganized conclusion is derived. Novel solutions and decisions that, on balance, are qualitatively better are detected.

Johnson and Johnson differentiated controversy from concurrence-seeking, which they defined as a process in which group members inhibit disagreement or the critique of an opposing position in order to reach agreement. In controversy there must be both cooperation and conflict.

The conditions under which productivity is increased through controversy are as follows:

(1) A cooperative goal structure exists through which information is accurately communicated; individuals feel safe enough to challenge each other's ideas; individuals value controversy rather than viewing it as a shortcoming; individuals are willing to deal with feelings as well as ideas and information; controversy is designed as win-win; and individuals recognize similarities in ideas as well as differences.

(2) There is heterogeneity of members. The greater the heterogeneity, the greater the amount of time members spend in controversy, thus the greater the productivity. Heterogeneity can exist in information, ability, reasoning strategies, and personality, as well as the more acknowledged differences of sex, race, background, and age.

(3) Relevant information is distributed among members. (*Relevant* in this case means "related to the task the group is working on.") If one

individual has all of the information, or if no one has relevant information, productivity will not be increased. However, the more information the group has distributed among its members the more productive the group will be.

(4) Members have the ability to disagree with each other without creating defensiveness. This condition is directly related to individuals' social skills. Two skills in particular are needed: (a) the ability "to disagree with each other's ideas while confirming each other's personal competence" (Johnson & Johnson, 1989, p. 102), and (b) the ability to take the perspective of the other, which was discussed above.

(5) Members have the ability to engage in rational argument. Engaging in rational argument implies that members keep an open mind, are willing to be influenced by the cogent arguments of others, are able to use logical reasoning and to determine when reasoning leads to valid conclusions, are themselves able to organize their reasoning to present to others, and so on.

When these conditions are present, controversy produces increased productivity and achievement over concurrence-seeking groups, competitive debate, or individuals working alone.

A final and hopeful note should be added to this discussion of Johnson and Johnson's work. They described a spiral in which trust is needed to achieve cooperation, but cooperation also leads to increased trust, which in turn leads to increased cooperation. In fact, the research shows that people seek out those with whom they have acted cooperatively, to again engage in cooperative action. Given the high correlation between cooperation and productivity, the spiral of cooperation may also be a spiral of productivity.

Freire: Transformation

Paulo Freire is a Brazilian educator whose lifelong work has been the education of illiterate adults in the Third World, both through his own practice and through the development of theory that has influenced educators worldwide. The antecedents of his theoretical ideas can be found in the thinking of Jean-Paul Sartre; Erich Fromm; Jose Ortega y Gasset; Mao Tse-tung; Martin Luther King, Jr.; and Che Guevara. These thinkers, coupled with his own remarkable sociopolitical insights, led him to not only understand the political potency of bringing literacy to the disenfranchised but to advocate for the legitimate right of all people to participate in creating their own culture and world. His work with illiterate peasants in Brazil so threatened the existing order that he was jailed and subsequently exiled. Much of his work in Latin America has been through UNESCO and the Chilean Institute for Agrarian Reform. Freire was himself born into poverty and experienced firsthand the disenfranchisement of the poor and oppressed.

For Freire dialogue is the process through which human beings collectively transform their world. That transformation involves altering their taken-for-granted assumptions about their world and their relationship to it. This transformation is not conceived of as a one-time change—that is, as a change from an incorrect position to a more correct one—but rather as integral to human development. It is the process of evolving new meaning as humans interact with their world in ways that change the world and are in turn changed by it. "To exist humanly, is to *name* the world, to change it" (Freire, 1970, p. 76). Dialogue, then, is a creative process, one in which meaning is created or re-created.

It is also a social process. Although meaning is constructed in the minds of individuals, it is through dialogue—the process of communicating, challenging, and affirming meaning—that the world is transformed. Naming the world, transforming it, is the way humans find significance, thus it is an "existential necessity." As such, it cannot be the privilege of an elite few but rather is the right of everyone. For this reason, the naming cannot be done alone, nor for others, for that robs them of their words.

Freire's use of the term *naming* is appropriate. To give a name to something, whether that something is a concrete object, a newly conceived concept, or an action, is a way of making it available for dialogue. As long as the "something" is taken for granted it is not available for dialogue. Likewise, renaming allows people to see a familiar something in a new way. Thus in proposing that all people have the right to participate in naming of the world, Freire is talking about the power to reconceptualize the world, to think in new ways about it.

Dialogue, according to Freire (1970, p. 75), is about both reflection and action: "To speak a true word is to transform the world." By transforming the world Freire means to alter it in ways that allow people to be more human. His emphasis in this quote is, however, on the term *true*. True words, spoken in dialogue with others, alter the world. This action and reflection occur simultaneously, not sequentially. In fact, Freire did not dichotomize acting and reflecting; together they are praxis.

Dialogue is also, according to Freire, not a technique used to help achieve some preferred result. Rather it is part of the historical progress of human beings becoming more human, more aware, and more conscious. However, for Freire, as for the other theorists I have discussed above, dialogue is not just talk; the term is reserved for a way of interacting that is more true, more open, more human.

Freire often referred to the "non-dialogic man," individuals who attempt to indoctrinate others, requiring them to adjust to a reality that is already defined.

What does dialogue require of people? Those who engage in dialogue must come to it with humility, love, faith, and hope—a formidable list of characteristics, but one that exemplifies a relational, rather than technique, perspective.

Humility. Freire (1994, p. 71) wrote eloquently about the need for humility in this passage from *Pedagogy of the Oppressed.*

> Dialogue cannot exist without humility. The naming of the world, through which people constantly re-create that world, cannot be an act of arrogance. Dialogue, as the encounter of those addressed to the common task of learning and acting, is broken if the parties (or one of them) lack humility. How can I dialogue if I always project ignorance onto others and never perceive my own? How can I dialogue if I regard myself as a case apart from others—mere "its" in whom I cannot recognize other "I"s? How can I dialogue if I consider myself a member of the in-group of "pure" men, the owners of truth and knowledge, for whom all non-members are "these people" or "the great unwashed"? . . . Someone who cannot acknowledge himself to be as mortal as everyone else still has a long way to go before he can reach the point of encounter. At the point of encounter there are neither utter ignoramuses nor perfect sages; there are only people who are attempting, together, to learn more than they now know.

Love. Freire (1970, pp. 77-78) wrote about dialogue as the creation and re-creation of meaning and suggests that creation is an act of love. Thus dialogue cannot exist in the absence of love of the world and of humankind. "Love is at the same time the foundation of dialogue and dialogue itself."

Faith. In addition to humility and love, those who engage in dialogue need faith in the ability of people to make and remake their world. This is not faith in an elite group who have shown some particular aptitude, nor faith in the well-educated who have developed a certain expertise, but rather faith in the ability of average human beings to comprehend their world and, with others, to transform their world. Freire (1970, p. 79) said, "Faith in man[kind] is an *a priori* requirement for dialogue; the 'dialogical man' believes in other men even before he meets them face to face. . . . Without this faith in man, dialogue is a farce which inevitably degenerates into paternalistic manipulation."

Hope. Freire said that dialogue requires hope. Without hope that things can change there is no need for dialogue. Hopelessness begets silence, not dialogue. If individuals do not expect anything to happen as a result of their dialogue, the dialogue will be empty and meaningless.

Critical thinking. Finally, dialogue requires individuals to engage in critical thinking. Freire differentiates critical thinking from naive thinking. Naive thinking sees the future as extrapolation from the past. The naive thinker's focus is on accommodation to the anticipated future, which is seen as inevitable. The critic, by contrast, is focused on the continued transformation of reality.

Practical Observations on Dialogue

Coming as they do from different disciplines, the theorists discussed above offer remarkably similar ideas about dialogue. Although some include ideas that the others do not, and there are clear differences among them, none basically contradicts the others.

The observations that I offer in this section are, in one sense, a summary of these theorists; in another sense, they represent my own view of dialogue, which has been informed by these thinkers but which is not limited to their ideas.

A Definition

In my view, dialogue is talk—a special kind of talk—that affirms the person-to-person relationship between discussants and which acknowledges their collective right and intellectual capacity to make sense of the world. Therefore, it is not talk that is "one way," such as a sales pitch, a directive, or a lecture; rather it involves mutuality and jointness. I do not want to suggest that dialogue is without emotion and passion or that it is without confrontation and challenge. It involves both, but within bounds that affirm the legitimacy of others' perspectives.

Dialogue has the potential to alter the meaning each individual holds and, by so doing, is capable of transforming the group, organization, and society. The relationship between the individual and the collective is reciprocal and is mediated through talk. People are both recipients of tacit assumptions and the creators of them. In this way dialogue results in the co-creation of meaning. The meaning that is created is shared across group members; a common understanding is developed. I am hesitant here to use the familiar word *consensus,* because it seems too restricted, limited to a decision-making process. I mean something more encompassing. The common understanding engendered by dialogue is one in which each individual has internalized the perspectives of the others and thus is enriched by a sense of the whole. Dialogue brings people to a new way of perceiving an issue that may be of concern to all. That new understanding might include what actions (decisions) should be taken individually and collectively, but such resulting actions are not its essence; its essence is that people have collectively constructed new meaning.

The Purpose of Dialogue

It is worthwhile to consider what purpose dialogue can serve (see Table 1). Argyris has defined the goal as uncovering one's own and the organization's unintentional errors that limit learning. Mezirow's goal has been emancipating individuals from the untested assumptions that limit their development as human beings. Johnson and Johnson took as their goal learning and productivity. The goal Bohm had in mind was shared meaning, which he believed people can come to by dissolving the programs that blind them. Finally, Freire's goal has been to transform the world through understanding and re-creating it. In all of these perspectives there is the intent to uncover that which is tacit—to become aware of the paradigm in which those individuals engaged in the dialogue are themselves embedded. By making manifest that which has been taken for granted, the participants in the dialogue are able to hold their assumptions up for examination and, when warranted, to construct new joint meaning that is tested against their reasoning.

The Role of Others in Learning

Dialogue occurs in a group setting. The group may be quite small, as in some of Argyris' and perhaps Johnson and Johnson's groups, but it is clear that Bohm and Freire were talking about larger groups, even forty or more. People often mistakenly think the prefix *dia* means "two" and thus think of a dialogue as only occurring between two people. But in its Greek origin *dia* means "passing through," as in *diathermy,* or "thoroughly" or "completely," as in *diagnosis.* Thus, dialogue is a social event, a community of people thinking together.

As each of these theorists has suggested, people need others to see what they cannot see for themselves. That is a difficult idea in a society steeped in individualism. To acknowledge that others are needed is the act of humility that Freire talked about or the acceptance of our vulnerability that Bohm referenced. People seem more comfortable with the idea that others can

— Table 1 —

Theorist	Purpose	Process	Skills and Attitudes	Target Audience
Argyris	To uncover one's own errors in reasoning and in so doing to uncover the defensive routines that prevent the organization, as a whole, from learning.	Raise issues on-line in small groups or through left- and right-hand column written cases to uncover individuals' reasoning so they have the choice to alter them. To create maps of the group's defensive routines for public discussion so that the group has the choice to alter them.	Model II skills of advocacy and inquiry, publicly testing inferences, offering one's reasoning and seeking disconfirmation.	Both individuals and the organizations of which they are a part.
Bohm	To develop "social intelligence"; to create the shared understanding (glue) that might better hold our fragmented society together.	Minimally structured dialogue in large groups of twenty or more which meet over several months. Groups are facilitated only initially.	Willingness to suspend one's own assumptions while reflecting on the ideas, feelings, and actions of the group.	Society as a whole.
Johnson and Johnson	To increase the learning and the concomitant productivity in groups.	Promotive interaction; face-to-face interaction in which individuals encourage each other to achieve, complete tasks, and produce in order to reach the group's goals.	Provide each other with effective help and feedback, exchange needed resources, challenge each other's conclusions and reasoning, act in trusting and trustworthy ways, advocate an exertion of effort to achieve mutual goals, be motivated to strive for mutual benefit, have a moderate level of arousal.	Groups who need to learn with and from each other; such as teams, class members, study groups.

Mezirow	To free individuals of the distorting assumptions imparted through institutions including government, corpora-tions, and education.	Deliberate on a topic to achieve a broad consensus of those who are informed, rational, and objective.	Be able to weigh evidence and assess arguments objectively; be open to alternate perspectives; be able to critically reflect on presuppositions and their consequences; accept informed, objective, and rational consensus as a legitimate test of validity.	Individuals and the institutions with which they interact which unknowingly impart distorted assumptions.
Freire	To free groups and individuals from the tacit assumptions that keep them oppressed.	Talk together in equal relationship without differentiated teaching and learning roles.	Humility, love, faith, hope, and critical thinking.	Populations that are oppressed by cultural norms and political processes.

provide them with *new information* than with the idea that they need others to put their own thinking to a test. Stephen Brookfield (1988) has said, "Trying to understand the motive for our actions or attempting to identify the assumptions undergirding our apparently objective, rational beliefs is like trying to catch our psychological tail. . . . We must hold our behavior up for scrutiny by others, and in their interpretation of our actions we are given a reflection, a mirroring of our own actions from an unfamiliar psychological vantage point."

People Already Know How to Have a Dialogue

Dialogue needn't be thought of as something unfamiliar or new. People already have the necessary skills. For example, most people can think of someone with whom they engage in a certain kind of conversation on a fairly consistent basis—perhaps a long-time colleague, a cherished friend, or a spouse. These are conversations in which each person works hard to grasp the perspective of the other, sensing that he or she is not being judgmental but rather trying to see the world through the other's eyes; each person has his or her thinking seriously challenged and seriously supported. This is dialogue, and although it may not always feel comfortable nor be satisfying in the moment, it is authentic in a way most work conversations are not. If people value such talk, it is in part because they value the individual with whom it takes place and recognize the value that that person places on them. People value the content of the dialogue as well, recognizing that they have grown and changed through it.

If one accepts this hypothesis, that people are capable of engaging in a dialogue without necessarily having to learn new skills or technique, then dialogue is more about the nature of the relationship between people than about the specific words they say or the technique they employ.

Dialogue Is a Relationship

When people talk with others they convey not only a content message but also who the others are in relation to themselves—for instance, that the others are equal, less knowledgeable, revered, or unimportant. That relationship is conveyed through what is said and what is withheld, the choice of words, tone, and nonverbal actions. The relationship expressed through dialogue is one in which the other is valued, trusted, and an equal whose ideas are respected if not always agreed with. People are in a person-to-person relationship with the other.

Freire's five requirements for dialogue cited above—humility, love, faith, hope, and critical thinking—are about the nature of the relationship between the speaker and those with whom the speaker is in dialogue. When Freire (1994, p. 71) said, "Self-sufficiency is incompatible with dialogue. Men and women who lack humility (or have lost it) cannot come to the people, cannot be their partners in naming the world," he was talking about how people view themselves in relationship to others.

Even in Argyris' more technical approach to dialogue, at the heart of Model II skills, there are the values of valid information, free and informed choice, and internal commitment to the choice. Argyris' values speak to the nature of the relationship between people—that is, that the intent of the individual should not be to use others, either purposefully or unwittingly, but rather to guard free and informed choice for both him- or herself and others.

I am suggesting here that dialogue is not a difference in technique but a difference in relationship. I seriously question whether more technique is necessary. There is already a great deal of technique that relates to clear feedback, supportive and clarifying statements, air time, paraphrasing to check out what is understood, and so on. That is not to say that people consistently make use of the technique that is available to them. But even when they do, they may not change their intent to manipulate or control. People may have altered their words but not the nature of their relationship to others.

Dialogue transpires in the context of relationship, and central to it is the idea that through interaction people acknowledge the wholeness, not just the utility, of others.

Dialogue Can Offset the Instrumental Nature of Work Relationships

The relationship built into much of the talk at work is instrumental—that is, the person with whom one is talking is viewed as a means to accomplish an objective. The term *human resource,* used as a synonym for organizational members, symbolizes the instrumental nature of relationships in organizations. To speak of people as a *resource* is to relegate them to the status of objects, comparable to equipment or supplies. The use of the term makes it possible to deny that the resource, the persons involved, are human beings with purposes and wills of their own. Even the term *employee* carries with it an instrumental flavor.

When Bohm eschewed agendas it was an attempt to avoid the instrumental relationships that agendas typically precipitate. Instrumental relationships are subject-object relationships rather than person-to-person relationships. In Martin Buber's (1970) words, "I-It" rather than an "I-Thou."

That said, it is clear that hierarchical structures in organizations are designed as a way to get work done through others. A manager's job, by definition, is instrumental and his or her relationship to subordinates is instrumental. If instrumental relationships are embedded in the way organizations are structured, is it not asking the impossible to encourage the holders of those positions to dialogue in a person-to-person relationship?

Perhaps what is necessary in organizations is to create opportunities to have frequent dialogue and through that dialogue to come to shared meaning. Then, with that co-created meaning as a foundation, individuals and groups could interact in more purposeful ways to make decisions and problem solve. I do not want to go so far as to say they would "engage in their normal way of interacting in business" because even when people interact in more purposeful ways than dialogue would support, it would be inconsistent to *use others as instruments* to accomplish a purpose without their full knowledge and uncoerced agreement with the purpose. In many organizations that caveat may not represent business as usual.

If there were frequent dialogue in our organizations, then the nature of people's relationships with each other might change. As Bohm (1992, p. 119) said, "When you listen to somebody else, whether you like it or not, what they say becomes part of you." Through dialogue it might be possible to alter taken-for-granted assumptions not only about what people are trying to accomplish together but also about how people structure their relationships. Putting collective intelligence to use, they might find some resolution to the management emphasis on instrumentality.

Dialogue Affirms the Intellectual Capability of Ordinary Human Beings

Dialogue is based on the principle that the human mind is capable of using logic and reason to understand the world, rather than having to rely on the interpretation of someone who claims authority through force, tradition, superior intellect, or divine right. The theorists considered here are not the only ones who have faith in the ability of human beings to comprehend their world. Such faith is at the heart of Reginald Revans' (1980) action-learning process. It is also in the Theory Y that Douglas McGregor (1960) suggested as an alternative to Theory X. More recently it is in the ideology that underlies Marvin Weisbord's (1992) advocacy of future search conferences (see Appendix A), as well as Merrelyn Emery's (1989) similar "whole system in a room" processes. And, of course, it underlies participative democracy.

Dialogue is an affirmation of the intellectual capability of not only the individual but also the collective. It acknowledges that everyone is blind to his or her own tacit assumptions and needs the help of others to see them. It acknowledges that each person, no matter how smart or capable, sees the world from a *perspective* and that there are other legitimate perspectives that could inform that view. People know this intellectually and yet have great difficulty living its reality. I am often struck by the language I hear when managers talk about such concepts as empowerment, participation, or even dialogue: "We want others to feel involved," not "We need the ideas of others"; "People will be more willing to change if they have had input into the change," not "We need the ideas of others to understand how to make the change." The emphasis in managers' language is more often on the manipulation of the perception of others than on the need for or use of their collective intellect. Perhaps this language reflects ambivalence or perhaps it reflects a partial step toward the use of the collective intelligence.

The Outcome of Dialogue Is Unpredictable

It is not possible to anticipate the outcome of dialogue; if it were, there would be no need to engage in it. Because meaning is co-created in the act of dialogue, it cannot be known ahead of time what meaning will emerge. It is possible that some taken-for-granted assumptions may be raised that management would prefer be left alone—for example the differential in salary between upper management and workers, the organization's effect on the environment, or the overall purpose of the organization.

It would, however, be inconsistent to say to a group in dialogue: "Examine the paradigms under which you function so that those that are limiting can be altered, but do not examine anything that touches on issues of power or control." If a forum is created in which dialogue can occur, it must be accepted that some of the beliefs that people hold sacred will be challenged.

The unpredictability of dialogue may be problematic in yet another sense. That is, when resources are allocated for an organizational effort such as dialogue, people typically want some assurance up front about what outcomes might be expected. To do less would not be seen as exercising fiscal responsibility. Yet no one can anticipate where dialogue might go.

Dialogue Is Paradoxical

The practice of dialogue depends upon the organization having a climate which is open and respectful of individuals and where information is shared, members are free from coercion, and everyone has equal opportunity to challenge the ideas of others. Without such a climate it is unlikely that either individuals or groups would expend the energy or incur the risks that would be needed for dialogue to take place. For example, it is unlikely that individuals would hold their opinions up for scrutiny in a climate where mistakes are seen as failure and the norm is to cover up what went wrong. It is equally unlikely that organizational members would challenge others if that challenge might be viewed as insubordination.

Thus a paradox exists: In order for organizational members to risk engaging in dialogue, the organization must have a climate that supports the development of individuals as well as the development of the organization; yet that climate is unlikely to come into being until individuals are able to engage in dialogue. The individual and the norms of the system are so intertwined that attempts to change either without changing the other are not likely to succeed. To the extent that either individual actions or system norms are tacit the change becomes even more difficult.

That said, the only place such a change *can* begin is with individuals—not the individual in isolation but individuals in community. When a group of individuals begins to change, even a nonsanctioned group, the organization has begun to change. Perhaps the first step in moving beyond the paradox is to name it—that is, to publicly identify the situation in which organizations find themselves, to raise it to the level of public discussion, of dialogue.

Examples of How Dialogue Can Be Incorporated into Work Processes

It is doubtful that, in most organizations, dialogue could immediately be part of the regularly scheduled Monday morning staff meeting. The norms for how people relate to each other, what they can and cannot say, who they are supposed to be, may be too strong to overcome. The problem, of course, is that it is difficult to put aside the power and mistrust that keeps people from engaging in dialogue in the first place. If everything but the talk stays the same—that is, who makes the decisions, who sets the limits, who has special access to knowledge—then how can people relate in a different way? It is, I think, too much to expect people to position dialogue on top of the existing structure and have it be unfeigned.

I am also skeptical dialogue can be promoted in the confines of a classroom or a retreat setting with any hope it will carry over to everyday work. Being in dialogue in the isolation of the classroom does not address or redress the many political and cultural issues that prevent people from being in dialogue in the worksite. Moreover, I am convinced that people do not need to "learn" to speak their own truth, that they already know how.

There appears, however, to be an emerging alternative. There are a number of new work processes that organizations are exploring, or inventing, that incorporate significant opportunities for dialogue—often in large-group settings. These include strategic search conferences, open space technology, real-time strategic change, and action-learning, to name a few of the most prominent. I want to refer to these collectively as *forums*. In each of these forums a kind of container or holding environment is created in which dialogue about critical organizational issues occurs over a period of several days. The purpose of these forums is not to engage in dialogue; rather dialogue is the vehicle through which work is examined and accomplished within the forum. That difference would appear to be an important one for organizational settings—that dialogue is a way of getting work done, not an end in itself.

Although critical work is accomplished, these forums are far from being "business as usual." The container or holding environment that is created incorporates many of the elements of dialogue that are proposed by the five theorists discussed in this paper. Thus, the forums embody fundamentally different conditions from those in which people usually talk with each other. It is also important to note that the forums address a specific issue that is critical to the organization such as a problem that needs solving or a strategy that needs to be developed. They are not exercises or hypothetical situations but the real work of the organization. The dialogue that ensues is about issues that participants care about and in which they have considerable stake.

My intent here is not to advocate these particular forums but to use them to illustrate how organizations may be incorporating dialogue in a more acceptable way. (I have placed a brief description of each of the forums in Appendix A.) Although these forums vary greatly in terms of such elements as method and size, they share a number of conditions that make dialogue viable.

First, top management agrees, well before the event, to relinquish power to the forum to make changes; it is not a situation where the group makes recommendations that management may take under advisement. What legitimizes this empowerment of the group is that all of the knowledge that exists in the organization about the issue being addressed is invited into the room. Furthermore, all of the knowledge that is in the room is available to everyone. When everyone comes to know what everyone else knows about the issue, a delay to seek a wider or more informed view is no longer valid. A forum in which such an up-front agreement has been made represents a fundamental change in the distribution of power and control in the organization, albeit a temporary one.

Second, in these forums measures are taken to reduce the effects of hierarchy because such effects have an acknowledged tendency to limit dialogue. Most of the forums are facilitated not by management but by a "third party." Often management does not play a central or visible role; there are no introductory speeches about the need to change or the importance of the task, and no closing remarks are made in appreciation of the effort of the troops. In some of these forums, management is not in the room at all; in others, management is present but has been coached to be parsimonious with its contributions. There is a strong component of self-management in the forums; process issues that arise are resolved in the small groups or in the total group. There are basic guidelines embodied in the structure of the forum (these vary with different types of forums) which are typically established at the beginning by consent of the whole, but these are often minimal and alterable. The diminished role of management and the focus on self-management significantly reduce the influence of status and rank and create an equality among participants that facilitates the dialogue.

Third, the assumption is made that the group that has come together is capable of both understanding and resolving the issue with which they are faced. There are no experts or consultants present to advise how the issue should be addressed. The necessary information and expertise, which are typically diverse, are embedded in the people in the room, who come from different parts of the organization and from multiple levels. Often customers and suppliers are invited, adding yet more diversity of perspective. It is the collective intelligence of the group, expressed through dialogue, that is sought as the source of new understanding. In referencing search conferences specifically, Weisbord (1992) said, "We believe the real world is knowable to ordinary people and their knowledge can be collectively and meaningfully organized. In fact, ordinary people are an extraordinary source of information about the real world" (p. 13). This willingness to trust in collective intelligence rather than "expert" opinion requires a major shift in thinking about where the "true" source of knowledge resides in organizations. In most organizations people are more comfortable with having experts construct an answer, although the need for everyone to discuss it and eventually "buy in" is acknowledged.

Fourth, these forums are often a mixture of small- and large-group interactions. The small groups provide the opportunity to participate that often does not exist in large groups. Yet the large group is critical to contain the sense of the whole. The alternation between small groups and the large group encourages individuals and functional groups to challenge, question, refute, and reflect and to hear others do the same. Yet the context is cooperative; there is an agreed-upon goal toward which the total group is striving and which the controversy serves. Forums occur over an extended period of time, often several days, allowing individuals to build the trust and respect for each other that can accommodate challenge. This mixture of challenge and cooperation may also represent a major shift in thinking from organizational norms in which questioning is considered resistance to change and challenge is acceptable only when it is directed downward.

I have called these forums a container and I think the figure is useful. It is as if people can experiment within this contained space; it is a place to try out things that are too risky to permit in day-to-day work. There is safety in the confines of the container where people agree to function differently but also agree to the time and space limits. Organizations may initially need these "contained" times and spaces where organizational members can experience what it is like to be in a different type of relationship with each other. Then, over time, perhaps the new way of talking, the new way of being with each other, can encroach into the day-to-day activities of the organization, so that the staff meeting or the planning meeting becomes more dialogic. If people can act in these "contained" spaces in ways that are more open and egalitarian, and if they can share power more fully, then, over time, the power and structure of the organization may shift and the organization may, in fact, develop.

These forums and techniques can lead to development of an organization by two means: first, by virtue of the content of the dialogue itself, and, second, by the nature of the interaction, which has the potential to alter the political and relationship structure of the organization.

With respect to the first means, the forums discussed here address a specific organizational issue. Through the dialogue that occurs, the collective intelligence of the organization is brought to bear on that issue. As Johnson and Johnson noted, the result is likely to be an understanding of the issue that is richer, more integrated, and more creative than any one individual or homogeneous group is likely to produce. This new understanding may lead to more productive actions and decisions. Additionally, each individual engaged in the dialogue is likely to come away with greater comprehension of the issue and thus a commitment to subsequent actions. I am proposing an outcome that is more complex than the truism that people will support what they have some say in. I suggest that it is not involvement that commits organizational members; rather it is (1) the engagement of their reasoning, (2) their mental wrestling with the complexity of the issue, and (3) the fuller understanding those mental processes produce that make the position arrived at more acceptable, regardless of whether it corresponds with one's own. The organization develops through the new understandings that are borne of the dialogue.

With respect to the second means, dialogue changes the nature of the interaction. Through dialogue, individuals experience themselves in different political relationships with each other. Engaging in a forum in which power has been transferred to the collective can lay the foundation for the group to question the status quo in which the collective is not so empowered. Organizational members might reason: "Clearly this group, as a whole, understands this issue better than any single individual or single group, regardless of their position in the organization. Why are we empowered around this issue and not others that are equally critical to us? Perhaps addressing critical issues collectively should be the norm."

Likewise, interacting as equals may lead organizational members to recognize that they are, in fact, equal in intellectual capability, reasoning, and knowledge and therefore that others have less right to special privileges or deference. They may come to question the basis which legitimizes others giving direction, receiving disproportional compensation, or withholding information.

Finally, self-managing the process of the forum may convince organizational members that they are capable of self-management in general and do not need experts or management to shepherd them through processes. They may come to believe in their own collective capability to design actions that lead to greater productivity and development.

The historical development of organizations has been in the direction of greater flexibility, adaptability, and ability to take into account a more comprehensive, and recently, a more global perspective. This development has come about through a consistent shift away from autocracy and bureaucracy and toward increased participation—a shift in the locus of power. As Peter Block (1993) said, "Often our focus on change is aimed at better communication, working as a team, meeting to decide how to cut costs, and giving recognition for exceptional contributions. These actions do not change the rules, they simply help us better adapt to the same game. For the game to change, hard currency has to change hands. In organizations, hard currency is rearranging who makes choices, who defines culture, who determines the measures, and who shares in the wealth" (p. 53). The forums discussed here allow organizational members to experience themselves in a different relationship with each other and with the whole of the organization; this opens the door to altering the fundamental power and structure in the organization.

I find the emergence of such forums a promising sign that our organizations are capable of becoming more dialogic. I am also encouraged that there seem to be a growing number of such forums in a variety of shapes and formats. However, I do not want to suggest that these forums are the only ways in which dialogue can emerge within organizations. There have certainly been other examples of organizational practices that point in the same direction—for instance, group meetings in which a "devil's advocate" is regularly appointed or project teams which purposively include a naive member to ask the taken-for-granted questions. These techniques are far from being dialogue as it is described here, yet they show a direction, a growing intent in organizations to institutionalize dialogue.

Conclusion

Dialogue offers organizations the possibility of developing individuals and systems that are better able to handle the complexity of this diverse and fast-changing world. But it is a nonscientific solution in an age in which people are most comfortable trusting science. It is a long-term solution at a time when people want immediate answers.

Yet it is consonant with other changes in organizations, such as empowerment, self-managed teams, and reduction in layers of management. This is an interesting age: It has one foot in the traditions of the past and one foot testing the ground of new ways to function. Dialogue is a tool of the new ground. It may also be a tool to help discover where the new ground lies.

Appendix A

Future Search Conferences

Marvin Weisbord (1992) has popularized a process, which he calls the *future search conference,* for involving the whole organization in the development of strategy. A typical search conference brings together thirty to eighty people for sixteen hours across three days. Together they engage in a series of tasks that involve exploring the organization's past, present, and preferred future. The process is basically a democratic one, reminiscent of town meetings. There are no lectures by experts nor vision statements by leadership. The purpose is to learn together about a preferred future and to make that future happen. Each part of the conference—past, present, and future—has four elements: (1) to build a database, (2) to look at it together, (3) to interpret what is found, and (4) to draw conclusions for action.

The three days of the future search conference are preceded by a lengthy period of planning. A small group, representative of the prospective participants, meets with the conference facilitators to select the attendees and to communicate the search purpose and plan. A conference typically involves a wide diversity of participants, including customers and suppliers. The conference itself is facilitated by a team trained in the conference model.

The work of the search conference alternates between the large group and teams of approximately eight. Some of the tasks are accomplished by homogeneous, functional teams, whereas other tasks are accomplished in mixed stakeholder teams. The teams self-manage their semi-structured dialogue. The intent of the dialogue is not to resolve conflicts but to find "common ground all can stand on without forcing or compromising" (Weisbord, 1992, p. 7). The search conference seeks "to hear and appreciate differences, not reconcile them" (p. 7).

There are conclusions drawn at three levels: those for individual use, which each individual keeps; those for the functional level, which are reviewed at the meeting by the department personnel; and those that go across functions, which are reviewed at the conference by the top-management group. At each level, action plans are drawn up and agreed to, based on the conclusions.

Open Space Technology

Open space technology is a meeting format developed by Harrison Owen. Its purpose is to create a space in which breakthrough ideas can emerge. An open space conference is held in a large room without much furniture but with a great deal of wall space to post ideas and notices. A typical conference lasts for two to three days. The essence of the conference is embedded in the rules Owen (1992) has constructed for it:

(1) There is no agenda, but there is a theme that is stated at the beginning of the conference.

(2) No one is in charge.

(3) The meeting starts with everyone standing or sitting in a circle where they can see each other.

(4) Each participant who chooses identifies an issue related to the theme for which he or she is willing to take responsibility for holding a discussion. The topic is announced and then posted so that others can join. The identification of topics continues until all ideas have been exhausted.

(5) When all the ideas are out, participants sign up for the groups that are of particular interest to them.

(6) The sponsor of each group convenes the group at the appointed time, leads the discussion, and takes notes.

(7) The notes from all of the meetings are typed into a bank of computers and made immediately available to everyone.

(8) Each day of the conference, the topic identification and subsequent discussions are continued.

(9) "The rule of two feet" says that if a participant is bored or has nothing to contribute to a group, he or she should "honor the group" and leave to join a group that is of more interest.

According to Owen, the lack of form allows ideas to take their own shape, undistorted by status or politics. The facilitation for open space involves little more than establishing the purpose initially and outlining the minimal open-space guidelines as listed above.

Action-learning

Action-learning is a process developed by Reginald Revans fifty years ago in the coal fields of England. He involved managers in the resolution of their own production problems, an unheard of idea in 1945. Action-learning has two goals: (1) to benefit the organization by addressing perplexing problems that have heretofore been unsolvable, and (2) to benefit individuals by making it possible for them to learn with and from others by discussing the difficulties each member of the action set experiences while working on a significant organizational problem.

A typical action-learning program begins with a large-group workshop of three to five days in length. Following the workshop, small groups are formed to address specific organizational problems. The groups meet with or without a facilitator on a weekly or biweekly basis over a lengthy period, perhaps six to nine months. The groups meet for a full or half day depending upon the nature of the problem and the constraints of the organization. Halfway through this time all the groups may come together again for three to five days to exchange information. A final meeting of three to five days is usually planned at the end.

The nature of the problems that the groups address is critical. First, they are problems that are important to the organization, not made-up exercises. Second, the problems are complex in nature, dealing with systemic organizational issues. Third, they are problems that are not amenable to expert solutions nor have ready-made right answers.

Action-learning differs from more typical cross-functional task forces in that action-learning groups are charged with learning from the problems they are solving; that means assumptions are challenged and actions are confronted. In conventional task teams the major goal is to address the problem; any learning that occurs is incidental. A second difference is that action-learning groups are charged with implementation as well as planning. Much of the learning from an action-learning problem comes from attempting to garner the support and face the problems inherent in implementation. A third difference is that action-learning groups address *unfamiliar* problems rather than problems in which they already have expertise, as might be more common in task forces or process-improvement teams. Addressing unfamiliar problems results in fresh perspectives being brought to bear on problems and provides individuals the opportunity to learn new ways to address problems.

Action-learning is based on adult-learning principles, which hold that: (1) managers learn best from each other, (2) managers learn from reflecting on how they are addressing real problems, (3) managers learn when they are able to question the assumptions on which their actions are based, and (4) managers learn when they receive accurate feedback from others and from the results of their problem-solving actions.

Likewise, action-learning is based on organizational principles that hold that: (1) organizational issues are solvable by organizational members who care about the issues and (2) organizational members who have not previously been involved in the issue can offer a fresh perspective that results in innovative solutions.

There are numerous variations of action-learning which have been successfully implemented in different organizations. Action-learning can vary in terms of the composition of the groups, that is, across organizations, functions, and departments. It can also vary in terms of the length of time and frequency with which groups meet.

Real-time Strategic Change

The use of the term *real time* refers to the simultaneous planning and implementation of change. This whole-system-in-the-room process addresses the current issues of the organization in terms of their interconnections with the entire organizational system. All or a critical mass of the people in an organization from all levels are involved, including key internal and external stakeholders. This widespread involvement serves three purposes:

(1) A data-rich, complex, clear, composite picture of the organization's reality can be constructed by integrating the many perspectives represented.

(2) Shared insights that emerge from this more informed view pave the way for establishing internal and external partnerships that previously would have made no sense when stakeholders operated solely out of their limited perspectives.

(3) All key stakeholders understand, accept, and can start to use these broad, whole-picture views in deciding how they want and need to do business in the future (Jacobs, 1994, p. 25).

Real-time strategic change involves up to 2,000 people in three-day meetings. The three days are based on having a flow of information from the individual, to the small group, to the whole group, and back again. To accomplish this, conference facilitators set task and time limits; however, the discussions that go on within the groups are not structured. The intent is to control the process, not the content. There is an emphasis on truth-telling and honesty.

Real-time strategic change involves a more active role of the organization's leadership than do some of the other forums described here. For example, the meeting begins with a welcome from the organization leadership to highlight the importance of the event and the power of the group to shape the organization's strategy; times are set aside for the leadership to respond to questions formulated by mixed-table discussions; and the leadership is tasked with constructing a strategy based on the data generated by the mixed groups.

Appendix B: The Conditions of Dialogue

In this appendix I have placed the major constructs of the theorists discussed above into two categories: *speech acts,* by which I mean what individuals who are engaging in dialogue actually do; and *situation variables,* which are the norms and conditions under which the speech acts are exercised. In developing this consolidated list, I have stated each construct in the language of one specific theorist and then attached to it the names of theorists who are in agreement with that construct; in some cases this may do disservice to the theorist whose language is not represented. Moreover, the first list is more heavily weighted with the ideas of Argyris and of Johnson and Johnson, who focused more on technique than Freire, Bohm, and Mezirow.

Speech Acts

(1) Provide others accurate and complete information including feelings that bear upon the issue (Argyris, Johnson and Johnson, Mezirow);

(2) advocate one's own position (Argyris, Johnson and Johnson);

(3) make the reasoning in one's own views explicit—say how one got from the data to one's conclusion (Argyris);

(4) invite others to critique or inquire into one's own reasoning (Argyris, Bohm);

(5) identify reasoning errors in others (Argyris, Johnson and Johnson);

(6) when someone's view differs from one's own, inquire into other's reasoning (Argyris, Bohm);

(7) confirm others' personal competence when disagreeing with their ideas (Johnson and Johnson);

(8) design ways to test competing views (Argyris);

(9) regard assertions (one's own and others) as hypotheses-to-be-tested (Argyris, Bohm);

(10) voice the perspective of others (Johnson and Johnson, Mezirow, Argyris);

(11) change position when others offer convincing data and rationale (Argyris, Johnson and Johnson);

(12) illustrate and publicly test inferences (Argyris);

(13) back up generalizations with concrete examples (Johnson and Johnson, Argyris);

(14) advocate the exertion of effort to achieve mutual goals (Johnson and Johnson);

(15) acknowledge similarities in ideas as well as differences (Johnson and Johnson);

(16) reflect critically upon presuppositions and their consequences (Mezirow, Argyris, Bohm, Freire);

(17) weigh evidence and assess arguments objectively (Mezirow).

Situation Variables

In dialogue,

(1) members feel free from coercion (Mezirow, Johnson and Johnson, Argyris, Bohm, Freire);

(2) participants have equal opportunity to participate—including the chance to challenge, question, refute, and reflect and to hear others do the same (Argyris, Johnson and Johnson, Bohm, Mezirow);

(3) participants are heterogeneous in terms of such factors as personality, sex, attitudes, diverse experiences, and ability levels (Johnson and Johnson);

(4) the context is cooperative, individuals feel it is safe to challenge each other, and controversy is viewed as constructive (Johnson and Johnson, Argyris);

(5) information and expertise are distributed among participants, and participants do not feel the need to defer to one individual (Johnson and Johnson, Freire);

(6) meetings are held without purpose or agenda (Bohm);

(7) groups have positive outcome interdependence (Johnson and Johnson);

(8) groups have means interdependence (Johnson and Johnson).

Bibliography

Ackoff, R. (1994). *The democratic corporation.* New York: Oxford University Press.

Argyris, C. (1990). *Overcoming organizational defenses: Facilitating organizational learning.* Boston: Allyn and Bacon.

Argyris, C. (1992). *On organizational learning.* Cambridge, MA: Blackwell.

Argyris, C. (1993). *Knowledge for action.* San Francisco: Jossey-Bass.

Argyris, C., Putnam, R., & Smith, D. M. (1985). *Action science.* San Francisco: Jossey-Bass.

Ashby, W. R. (1957). *An introduction to cybernetics.* New York: Wiley.

Ashby, W. R. (1960). *Design for a brain.* New York: Wiley.

Barrentine, P. (Ed.). (1993). *When the canary stops singing.* San Francisco: Berrett-Koehler.

Berger, P. L., & Lockmann, T. (1966). *The social construction of reality.* New York: Doubleday.

Block, P. (1993). *Stewardship.* San Francisco: Berrett-Koehler.

Bohm, D. (1985). *Unfolding meaning: A weekend of dialogue with David Bohm.* New York: Ark Paperbacks.

Bohm, D. (1990). *On dialogue* (transcription). Ojai, CA: David Bohm Seminars.

Bohm, D. (1992). (interview by John Briggs). Dialogue as a path toward wholeness. In M. Weisbord (Ed.), *Discovering common ground* (pp. 111-124). San Francisco: Berrett-Koehler.

Brookfield, S. D. (1988). *Developing critical thinkers.* San Francisco: Jossey-Bass.

Buber, M. (1970). (Trans. by Walter Kaufmann). *I and thou.* New York: Charles Scribner's Sons.

Commons, M. L., Richards, F. A., & Armon, C. (Eds.). (1984). *Beyond formal operations: Late adolescent and adult cognitive development.* New York: Praeger.

Deutsch, M. (1949). An experimental study of the effects of co-operation and competition upon group process. *Human Relations, 2,* 199-231.

Emery, M. (Ed.). (1989). *Participative design for participative democracy.* Canberra: Centre for Continuing Education, Australian National University.

Freire, P. (1970). *Pedagogy of the oppressed.* New York: Seabury Press.

Freire, P. (1994). *Pedagogy of the oppressed* (Rev. ed.). New York: Continuum Publishing.

Gronn, P. C. (1983). Talk as the work: The accomplishment of school administration. *Administrative Science Quarterly, 28*(1), 1-21.

Handy, C. (1989). *The age of unreason.* Boston: Harvard Business School Press.

Jacobs, R. W. (1994). *Real time strategic change.* San Francisco: Berrett-Koehler.

Johnson, D. W., & Johnson, R. T. (1989). *Cooperation and competition: Theory and research.* Edina, MN: Interaction Book Company.

Jung, C. (1963). *Memories, dreams, reflections.* New York: Vintage Books.

Kegan, R. (1994). *In over our heads.* Cambridge, MA: Harvard University Press.

Kotter, J. P. (1990). *A force for change.* New York: Free Press.

Kuhn, T. S. (1962). *The structure of scientific revolution* (2nd ed.). Chicago: University of Chicago Press.

Labouvie-Vief, G. (1984). Logic and self-regulation from youth to maturity: A model. In M. L. Commons, F. A. Richards, & C. Armon (Eds.), *Beyond formal operations: Late adolescent and adult cognitive development.* New York: Praeger.

Lorde, A. (1984). *Sister outsider.* Freedom, CA: The Crossing Press.

McGregor, D. (1960). *The human side of enterprise.* New York: McGraw-Hill.

Mezirow, J. (1991). *Transformative dimensions of adult learning.* San Francisco: Jossey-Bass.

Mintzberg, H. (1973). *The nature of managerial work.* Englewood Cliffs, NJ: Prentice Hall.

Owen, H. (1992). *Riding the tiger: Doing business in a transforming world.* Potomac, MD: Abbott Publishing.

Perry, W. G. (1970). *Forms of intellectual and ethical development in the college years: A scheme.* New York: Holt, Rinehart & Winston.

Revans, R. (1980). *Action learning: New techniques for management.* London: Blond & Briggs.

Stewart, R. (1985). *The reality of management* (2nd ed.). London: Heinemann.

Weisbord, M. (1992). *Discovering common ground.* San Francisco: Berrett-Koehler.

CENTER FOR CREATIVE LEADERSHIP PUBLICATIONS

SELECTED REPORTS:

Beyond Work-Family Programs J.R. Kofodimos (1995, Stock #167) $25.00

CEO Selection: A Street-smart Review G.P. Hollenbeck (1994, Stock #164) $25.00

Coping With an Intolerable Boss M.M. Lombardo & M.W. McCall, Jr. (1984, Stock #305) $10.00

The Creative Opportunists: Conversations with the CEOs of Small Businesses
J.S. Bruce (1992, Stock #316) $12.00

Creativity in the R&D Laboratory T.M. Amabile & S.S. Gryskiewicz (1987, Stock #130) $12.00

The Dynamics of Management Derailment M.M. Lombardo & C.D. McCauley (1988, Stock #134). $12.00

Eighty-eight Assignments for Development in Place: Enhancing the Developmental
Challenge of Existing Jobs M.M. Lombardo & R.W. Eichinger (1989, Stock #136) $15.00

Enhancing 360-degree Feedback for Senior Executives: How to Maximize the Benefits and
Minimize the Risks R.E. Kaplan & C.J. Palus (1994, Stock #160) $15.00

An Evaluation of the Outcomes of a Leadership Development Program C.D. McCauley &
M.W. Hughes-James (1994, Stock #163) $35.00

Evolving Leaders: A Model for Promoting Leadership Development in Programs C.J. Palus &
W.H. Drath (1995, Stock #165) $20.00

Feedback to Managers, Volume I: A Guide to Evaluating Multi-rater Feedback Instruments
E. Van Velsor & J. Brittain Leslie (1991, Stock #149) $20.00

Feedback to Managers, Volume II: A Review and Comparison of Sixteen Multi-rater
Feedback Instruments E. Van Velsor & J. Brittain Leslie (1991, Stock #150) $80.00

Forceful Leadership and Enabling Leadership: You Can Do Both R.E. Kaplan (1996, Stock #171) $20.00

Gender Differences in the Development of Managers: How Women Managers Learn From
Experience E. Van Velsor & M. W. Hughes (1990, Stock #145) $35.00

A Glass Ceiling Survey: Benchmarking Barriers and Practices A.M. Morrison, C.T. Schreiber,
& K.F. Price (1995, Stock #161) $20.00

High Hurdles: The Challenge of Executive Self-development R.E. Kaplan, W.H. Drath, &
J.R. Kofodimos (1985, Stock #125) $15.00

The Intuitive Pragmatists: Conversations with Chief Executive Officers J.S. Bruce
(1986, Stock #310) $12.00

Key Events in Executives' Lives E.H. Lindsey, V. Homes, & M.W. McCall, Jr.
(1987, Stock #132) $65.00

Leadership for Turbulent Times L.R. Sayles (1995, Stock #325) $20.00

Learning How to Learn From Experience: Impact of Stress and Coping K.A. Bunker &
A.D. Webb (1992, Stock #154) $30.00

A Look at Derailment Today: North America and Europe J. Brittain Leslie & E. Van Velsor
(1996, Stock #169) $25.00

Making Common Sense: Leadership as Meaning-making in a Community of Practice
W.H. Drath & C.J. Palus (1994, Stock #156) $15.00

Managerial Promotion: The Dynamics for Men and Women M.N. Ruderman, P.J. Ohlott, &
K.E. Kram (1996, Stock #170) $15.00

Off the Track: Why and How Successful Executives Get Derailed M.W. McCall, Jr., &
M.M. Lombardo (1983, Stock #121) $10.00

Perspectives on Dialogue: Making Talk Developmental for Individuals and Organizations
N.M. Dixon (1996, Stock #168) $20.00

Preventing Derailment: What To Do Before It's Too Late M.M. Lombardo &
R.W. Eichinger (1989, Stock #138) $25.00

The Realities of Management Promotion M.N. Ruderman & P.J. Ohlott (1994, Stock #157) $20.00

Redefining What's Essential to Business Performance: Pathways to Productivity,
Quality, and Service L.R. Sayles (1990, Stock #142) $20.00

Succession Planning L.J. Eastman (1995, Stock #324) $20.00

Training for Action: A New Approach to Executive Development R.M. Burnside &
V.A. Guthrie (1992, Stock #153) $15.00

Traps and Pitfalls in the Judgment of Executive Potential M.N. Ruderman & P.J. Ohlott
(1990, Stock #141) $20.00

Twenty-two Ways to Develop Leadership in Staff Managers R.W. Eichinger & M.M. Lombardo
(1990, Stock #144) $15.00
Upward-communication Programs in American Industry A.I. Kraut & F.H. Freeman
(1992, Stock #152) $30.00
Using an Art Technique to Facilitate Leadership Development C. De Ciantis (1995, Stock #166)... $30.00
Why Executives Lose Their Balance J.R. Kofodimos (1989, Stock #137) $20.00
**Why Managers Have Trouble Empowering: A Theoretical Perspective Based on
Concepts of Adult Development** W.H. Drath (1993, Stock #155) $15.00

SELECTED BOOKS:

Balancing Act: How Managers Can Integrate Successful Careers and Fulfilling Personal Lives
J.R. Kofodimos (1993, Stock #247) $27.00
Beyond Ambition: How Driven Managers Can Lead Better and Live Better R.E. Kaplan,
W.H. Drath, & J.R. Kofodimos (1991, Stock #227) $29.95
**Breaking the Glass Ceiling: Can Women Reach the Top of America's Largest Corporations?
(Updated Edition)** A.M. Morrison, R.P. White, & E. Van Velsor (1992, Stock #236A) $13.00
Choosing to Lead (Second Edition) K.E. Clark & M.B. Clark (1996, Stock #327) $25.00
Developing Diversity in Organizations: A Digest of Selected Literature A.M. Morrison &
K.M. Crabtree (1992, Stock #317) $25.00
**Discovering Creativity: Proceedings of the 1992 International Creativity and Innovation
Networking Conference** S.S. Gryskiewicz (Ed.) (1993, Stock #319)... $30.00
Executive Selection: A Look at What We Know and What We Need to Know
D.L. DeVries (1993, Stock #321)... $20.00
**Healing the Wounds: Overcoming the Trauma of Layoffs and Revitalizing Downsized
Organizations** D.M. Noer (1993, Stock #245).. $27.50
If I'm In Charge Here, Why Is Everybody Laughing? D.P. Campbell (1984, Stock #205) $8.95
If You Don't Know Where You're Going You'll Probably End Up Somewhere Else
D.P. Campbell (1974, Stock #203)... $9.40
Inklings: Collected Columns on Leadership and Creativity D.P. Campbell (1992, Stock #233)....... $15.00
Leadership: Enhancing the Lessons of Experience (Second Edition) R.L. Hughes, R.C. Ginnett,
& G.J. Curphy (1996, Stock #266)... $49.95
The Lessons of Experience: How Successful Executives Develop on the Job M.W. McCall, Jr.,
M.M. Lombardo, & A.M. Morrison (1988, Stock #211) $22.95
Making Diversity Happen: Controversies and Solutions A.M. Morrison, M.N. Ruderman, &
M. Hughes-James (1993, Stock #320) $25.00
The New Leaders: Guidelines on Leadership Diversity in America A.M. Morrison
(1992, Stock #238) $29.00
Readings in Innovation S.S. Gryskiewicz & D.A. Hills (Eds.) (1992, Stock #240) $25.00
Selected Research on Work Team Diversity M.N. Ruderman, M.W. Hughes-James, &
S.E. Jackson (Eds.) (1996, Stock #326) $24.95
Take the Road to Creativity and Get Off Your Dead End D.P. Campbell (1977, Stock #204) $8.95
Whatever It Takes: The Realities of Managerial Decision Making (Second Edition)
M.W. McCall, Jr., & R.E. Kaplan (1990, Stock #218) $30.40
**The Working Leader: The Triumph of High Performance Over Conventional Management
Principles** L.R. Sayles (1993, Stock #243)... $24.95

SPECIAL PACKAGES:

Conversations with CEOs (includes 310 & 316) $16.00
Development & Derailment (includes 136, 138, & 144) $25.00
The Diversity Collection (includes 145, 236, 238, 317, & 320) $85.00
Executive Selection Package (includes 141, 321, & 157) $32.00
Feedback to Managers: Volumes I & II (includes 149 & 150) $85.00
Personal Growth, Taking Charge, and Enhancing Creativity (includes 203, 204, & 205) $20.00

Discounts are available. Please write for a comprehensive Publications catalog. Address your
request to: Publication, Center for Creative Leadership, P.O. Box 26300, Greensboro, NC 27438-
6300, 910-545-2805, or fax to 910-545-3221. All prices subject to change.